DIGITALIZATION AND THE FIELD OF AFRICAN STUDIES

Mirjam de Bruijn

DIGITALIZATION AND THE FIELD OF AFRICAN STUDIES

Carl Schlettwein Lecture 12
Basler Afrika Bibliographien

© 2019 The authors
© 2019 Basler Afrika Bibliographien
Basler Afrika Bibliographien
Namibia Resource Centre & Southern Africa Library
Klosterberg 23
P. O. Box
CH 4051 Basel
Switzerland
www.baslerafrika.ch

CARL SCHLETTWEIN
STIFTUNG

The Basler Afrika Bibliographien is part of the Carl Schlettwein Foundation

Cover image: Phone credit seller in Ntarinkom, Bamenda
(Sjoerd Sijsma 2010)
Editors: Veit Arlt, Jacob Geuder, Sarah Thiele
Layout and typesetting: Tilo Richter
ISBN 978-3-905758-98-6
ISSN 2297–7058

FOREWORD

The Carl Schlettwein Lecture 2017 marked a very special moment in the history of the Centre for African Studies Basel. This was the opening of the 7th European Conference on African Studies (ECAS), which was held at the University of Basel from 29 June to 1 July 2017. In cooperation with the Swiss Society for African Studies the Centre organized and hosted this largest event within African Studies in Europe on behalf of AEGIS, the European Network of African Studies Centers. Mirjam de Bruijn, Professor of Contemporary History and Anthropology of Africa at the University of Leiden, was an ideal choice for this distinguished lecture.

In her work, de Bruijn straddles disciplines, History and Anthropology, and uses this interdisciplinary perspective to cast a look at a vast array of topics: nomadism, youth and children, social (in)security, poverty, marginality, social and economic exclusion, violence, human rights and, of course, Information and Communication Technologies (ICTs). These topics all resonated in the theme of ECAS: Urban Africa – Urban Africans: New encounters of the rural and the urban. In fact, they describe the properties of African urban settings bringing to our attention how our scholarly endeavor is shaped by an interest in the way things came to be the way they are (History), on the one hand, and how they locally produce the conditions of their own intelligibility (Anthropology), on the other.

Through her work, Mirjam de Bruijn is at home in many parts of West Africa, especially in Tchad, Mali and

Cameroon. She is what she does research on: a nomad, a mobile person, but also a product of the world we live in. This world does not consist of foreign lands and home, but rather of foreigners roaming homes. A statement attributed to Saint Augustine says: "The world is a book and those who do not travel read only one page." De Bruijn has not only read, but also produced many pages, which the current generation of anthropologists of Africa is reading with a lot of benefit. She has, by her own account, but also by what she claims to be her politically inspired and engaged choice of subject, brought countless pages of what many perceived as the margins to the center of their world. In doing so, she offers us glimpses of worlds far away from the immediacy of the narcissist gaze shaping how we seek to retrieve the world in the social sciences. Mirjam de Bruijn, is a formidable fellow traveler helping us make sense of the ways we came to have a world of margins and centers.

Elísio Macamo
Basel, June 20 2018

DIGITALIZATION AND THE FIELD OF
AFRICAN STUDIES

Urbanization in Africa means rapid technological change. At the turn of the 21st century mobile telephony appeared in urban Africa, ten years later it covered large parts of rural Africa and, thanks to the smartphone, also became the main access point to the internet. These technological transformations in digitalization are supposed to bridge the gap between the urban and the rural, blurring the border that separates them. This occurs through the creation of economic opportunities and information flows that influence people's definition of self, of belonging, and of citizenship. These changes are greeted with great optimism. The message of Information and Communications Technologies for Development (ICT4D) for Africa has been one of glory and revolution. Practice, however, shows other sides. Increasingly, academic publications show that we are facing a new form of digital divide in which Africa is, again, at the margins.

These transformations influence the relations between urban and rural Africa and between 'Africa' and the World. Hence, the field of African Studies is influenced, both in its objects and in its forms of knowledge production, and in the formulation of the problems that we should study. In this lecture, I reflect on the past two decades of my research experience in West and Central Africa and how, for me, the field has changed. How can I translate these experiences into a form of critical knowledge production, and how does the study of technological change inform the redefinition of African studies for the 21st century?

SETTING THE SCENE

When I started research on mobile telephony in West and Central Africa in 2006, I had no idea where this would lead me. By then I had already been doing research in the region for 18 years. Still, it was a step into a vast, endless ocean with no horizon in sight, into a rapidly changing environment that felt and feels like being in a laboratory and making discoveries all the time. Nothing seemed to be the same on return trips. Until even today, I am struggling with the digitalization of my research field and research in itself. What are the social, political and economic consequences, and how do they translate into our practices as academics?

In 2006, when I had just begun my research into the social and political change in relation to Information and Communication Technologies (ICT), I was telephoned at breakfast time as I was about to have a cup of coffee in my home in the Netherlands. It was my friend Ahmadou, a herdsman, who called me on his Nokia phone from a cattle camp in central Mali. I could not have imagined that he would later become influenced by 'Jihadist' movements that occupied the region where he lived in 2012. Sympathy for this movement was also a consequence of fighters' videos and preachers' audio recordings that circulated on the smartphones of his younger siblings and son. In 2006, this was unthinkable. His political agency has transformed in the digital environment that the Sahel is now part of.

Figure 1: Ahmadou in his cattle camp (picture: Mirjam De Bruijn 2010).

This experience is part of the many 'discoveries' that I made over the past 11 years. I was lucky to receive two grants to work on research programs that investigated the technological changes in the field of communication in Africa. In the first program, Mobile Africa revisited (2006—2013), we concentrated on mobile phones as voice communicators in relation to socio-economic change. The second program, Connecting in times of duress (2012—2018), is geared towards mobile internet, smartphones, and the political landscape.[1]

In this text, I will share my wonder and amazement and relate these to new directions in African Studies. How did the digitalization of our environment change social and political processes, both in African societies and in the field of the qualitative study of these societies? Will it lead to a practice in which old hierarchies in knowledge production fade away? Will the citizen, the herdsman, and the youth all become equal partners in the digital space and in the mutual exchange of knowledge? Digitization of African studies as a field of practice and reflection is the challenge ahead of us. It offers unprecedented opportunities for de-hierarchization of the field.

With these questions, I also refer to the pioneering work of Carl Schlettwein, whose ideas about archiving and sharing knowledge have laid the foundation to develop critical knowledge production as a field. I am honored to write this text in his name.[2]

What I argue is that the digital environment offers qualitative researchers a new challenge with regard to critical knowledge production.[3] It allows for new forms of collaboration in which we can include alternative forms of writing, as well as audios and visuals, deepening research and expanding publication. It enables us to bridge. This bridging can connect scholars who are based in different parts of the world. But it is also a bridging with those we would normally call our 'informants'. In my view, the position of informants will radically change in the digital future. Academia will have to embrace the idea of 'real' co-production, or co-creation of knowledge, that includes other knowledge fields, like the arts and journalism, but certainly also the informant as *citizen scientist*.[4]

I will take you through some of my thoughts on the dynamics of digitalization of communication, that is, the introduction of mobile phones and smartphones. I concentrate on communication and information as the building blocks to understand the effects of digitalization. From these societal processes and socio-political change I distill dynamics that we can, in turn, apply to the practice of African Studies. The digitalization of knowledge will have revolutionary effects.

AFRICA'S DIVERSITY

In discussions on Africa and digitalization, the debate often unfolds around what is labeled 'digital divide' and indicates the separation of Africa from the world in terms of technological advancement. Maps documenting this divide depict the regions where I work in West and Central Africa as 'not connected' (see Figure 2). In this text, I will show the opposite. My interpretations of processes of change are based on those that I have observed and cannot be generalized. We must keep in mind that Africa is not a country (#Africaisnotacountry)! All understandings of 'Africa' should deal with diversity. When we speak about the digital and Africa, we should be aware of the wide diversity of connectivity. Nigeria, Gabon, Kenya, and South Africa are among the best connected countries on the continent, while Chad and the Central African Republic (CAR) are among the least connected. Add to this internal diversity between rural and urban areas, or between classes and genders that define the divide. It is therefore difficult to draw general conclusions. This text should be read as a reflection on my research experience in West and Central Africa. I am trained as an Anthropologist, work in the History Institute and African Studies Centre of Leiden University

Figure 2: World map of internet access (source: World Bank).

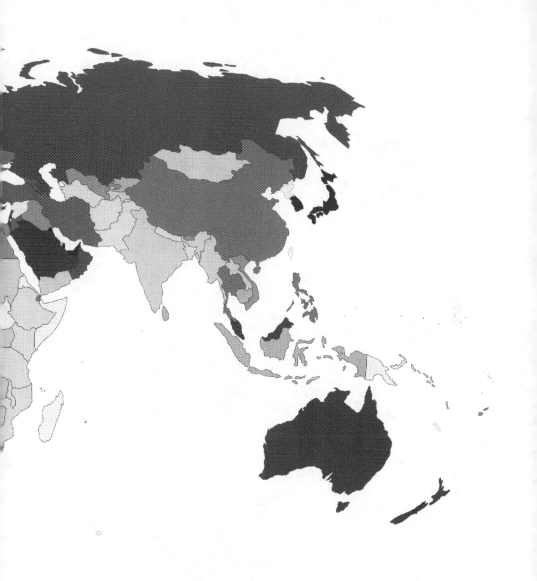

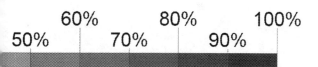

50% 60% 70% 80% 90% 100%

Figure 3: GSM coverage in the year 2001 (source: International Telecommunication Union).

Figure 4: GSM coverage in the year 2013 (source: International Telecommunication Union).

and, in my research, have been concentrating on digitalization and knowledge production since 2006.

COMMUNICATION REVOLUTION

Let us quickly scrutinize the communication landscape and the digital. The growth from the Global System for Mobile Communications (GSM) connectivity has been tremendous over the past 17 years (see Figures 3 and 4). Since the liberalization of the communications market, international companies have covered the ICT needs of Africans. ICT has become one of the growing sectors of the economy, comparable in terms of income to other major industries like gold and diamond mining.

The rapid growth of mobile telephony in Africa is a one in a series of revolutions in communication on the African continent, preceded by the introduction of script, roads, radio, and television. It differs from these other revolutions in communication in its tremendous speed and reach. Although one can imagine that the introduction of the radio and television had a profound effect on the quality and quantity of information that reached citizens, the vast amount of information and especially the rapid growth of voice communication through mobile technology is quite unique. Within a decade, first cities, then rural areas, were connected. Indeed, in the period between 2006 and 2013, the regions where I conducted my research (central Chad, central Mali, and Cameroon) saw an enormous leap forward in communication. From the start, users and scholars alike predicted its revolutionary effects.

The reported use of voice phone in Bamenda, Cameroon in 2010 illustrates the variety of functions for users, which range from affecting social relations and news distribution to creating affective ties to the device itself. Users cited ease of communication, contact with their children, access to "good news" and radio, or referred to the phone as a friend. One individual stated that the phone "is the good thing the whites have brought."[5]

People acknowledge the social change the voice phone brought to their lives, even before the arrival of smartphones equipped with internet access. Their remarks are reflected in the following citation:

> What the telegraph accomplished in a year the telephone has done in months. (...)
>
> The result can be nothing less than a new organization of society – a state of things where every individual, however secluded, will have at call every other individual in the community, to the saving of no end of social and business complications, of needless going to and fro, of disappointments, delays, and a countless host of those great and little evils and annoyances.
>
> The time is close at hand when the scattered members of civilized communities will be as closely united (...) as the various members of the body now are by the nervous system.[6]

This conclusion could belong to the research program *Mobile Africa revisited*;[7] it belongs, however, to a study done in 1880 that researched the effects of fixed phone lines in North America.

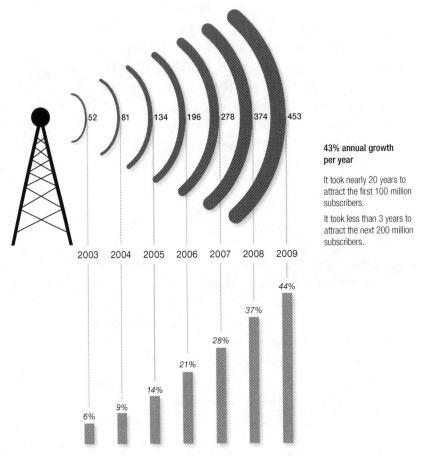

Figure 5: Africa's mobile phone market, 2010 (picture: Informa Telecoms & Media).

I include this citation as a reminder to be wary of thinking in terms of revolution and to make comparisons with earlier periods of 'communication revolutions' like the introduction of scripts and then books.[8] However, it cannot be denied that new ICTs have changed the speed of communication[9] and, as such, decreased distances and enabled rapid transfer of voice and knowledge, or information flows.[10] Such technological changes have an important impact and influence on social and economic life.

Mobile telephony has influenced many domains of life, as was already demonstrated in the statements of the Cameroonians. In the following section, I will go into the dynamics it brought to economic, social, and transfer of knowledge fields.

BUSINESS

I would first of all relate the rise in mobile communication to the fact that there has been a rush of international companies who saw their chance to enter a new market. It is clear that the liberalization of the communication market at the end of the last century is probably the most important factor in the increase in communication technology. The erection of cell phone towers is not a very costly endeavor. It allows many people to connect, and all the small amounts paid for each call add up to high profits for these companies. Individual states profit from the taxes levied on both the calls and the companies. The business model has been compared to that of a gold mining enterprise. This was in fact confirmed during an interview with a technician from the mobile company Zain in (then southern) Sudan in 2007. He was part of the team installing masts in southern Sudan and said: "… it is a good endeavor that will lead the company to the customers [who pay], exploring the poverty[11] market".[12] In those early days of mobile telephony, it was sold as a development enterprise. The next step foreseen by the CEO of Zain, a company based in Kuwait, was to connect over borders. This company, then in negotiation to take over the Dutch company Celtel, changed hands two times. Huge profits flow into the pockets of these companies that are usually based outside of Africa. Cases of local companies successfully developing into lucrative businesses are rare. In Mali, the market is dominated by Orange, a French company. In Cameroon, a South African company, MTN, rules. And in Chad, the market has two main operators: Airtel (former Celtel), an Indian Company, and Tigo, which is based in Italy. These companies have literally taken over the streets of Africa's cities with their colorful advertisements, the many small phonebooths and shops that have been set up everywhere, and, of course, the people phoning in the streets or simply carrying their phones.

The sporadic protests against user fees in Cameroon the high costs of mobile telephony and connectivity in Chad that became a fierce discussion in Facebook exchanges, the rising concerns of spending too much money on telephones—these are all indicators that whatever the 'phone revolution' does, it is foremost a commercial and business enterprise, bringing profit to international companies and authoritarian regimes while exploiting users. Nevertheless, it is a useful development.

VOICE

The first years of mobile telephony were the years of voice. Hans Peter Hahn and Lubovic Kiboora have relat-

Figure 6: Mast near the camp of Ahmadou, central Mali (picture: Mirjam De Bruijn 2010).

ed the rapid adoption of mobile telephony to the oral culture of 'African' societies.[13] I rather link the former to a need for communication in a globalizing world that has its precedents in African mobile cultures. When we analyze the mobility of people and their communities in Cameroon, Chad, and Mali, it seems rather logical that mobile communication followed in the footsteps of old forms of communication. These were mainly modes of travel as fixed lines were expensive and roads were often in disarray when they could be found at all, which was seldom the case in more remote regions. Sociality and economic relations flowed more easily with the regular possibility to connect through voice.[14]

Indeed, these early years of mobile communication with the support of new ICTs showed a clear change in social relations and a reinforcement of existing relationships. The tendency is that mobile communication reinforces strong ties in networks and makes weak ties less important. Granovetter's theory[15] points out that this development carries the risk of creating communities whose borders are not national, but ethnic and transnational.[16]

These new social constellations did not eradicate hierarchies. Mobile phone communication followed old models of communication and, in some cases, enhanced existing power relations in the same way the organization of diasporic networks did. An example of the latter is the case of the Chief of Baaba in the grassfields of Cameroon who controlled a network of diaspora countrymen for whom this direct link made it impossible to escape payments to the King. At the same time, however, it introduced entirely new power relations. Those who were able to control the new forms of communication, like the owners of mobile phone shops and booths, gained a new position in society.[17] The general effects of these types of linkages have been reinforced by existing structures, compartmentalization along ethnic and sometimes religious lines, and ultimately a reconfiguration of the social map of our world.

From 2009 onwards, voice communication and its technologies gradually disappeared and made way for smart technology. The introduction of the smartphone marked a new epoch of information and communication possibilities.

Figure 7: An abandoned phone booth, Cameroon (picture: Mirjam De Bruijn 2010).

FURTHERING THE DIGITAL

With the advancement of technology, more forms of connectivity are introduced. The arrival of the smartphone has been an important step in this regard. Previously, internet connectivity was limited to cyber cafés, university campuses, high-end hotels, and some private companies. The connectivity was of poor quality. High fiber connections never really reached the areas where I worked, not even in capital cities. The title of a 2013 CNN article 'The real mobile revolution: Africa's smartphone future' is telling.[18] In particular, cheap smartphones produced in China conquered the African market. By 2009, the Tecno phones that contain free and light versions of Facebook (included when one buys the phone) were popular in central Chad. Just a few years earlier, in 2003, I could only phone with a Thuraya, a satellite phone, and it was very expensive. Now, communication between the PhD students in our team, based in Holland and Chad, is easily accomplished with Facebook Messenger. More recently, the possibility to buy data packages in the size of gigabytes for internet use have increased the possibilities of the phone revolution. Voice was combined with many other techniques.

INFORMATION AND 'INFORMATION WORK'

In his book *The Information: A History, A Theory, A Flood*, Gleick gives an overview of how information has always been an engine of social change.[19] In communication theory, information consists of dots and stripes; it is a technique. However, through this technique, meaning and content travel and reach people who are connected through these techniques. These channels of information allow the shaping of meanings that have the power to influence societal change.

- Information is a collection of facts from which a conclusion can be drawn.
- Information is a message received and understood.

What is traveling by way of the technique of dots and stripes has meaning. Information is not neutral, just as the carrier of information is not neutral. Information is a dynamic process. We can compare it with Johannes Fabian's understanding of memory as 'memory work'.[20] It is constant interpretation, sending, choice making, and remembering that make information a complex and highly social and politically informed 'thing' that may have the capacity to transform. It is an active process. This is especially what it has become in new internet fora and platforms in cyberspace. This is certainly also a process in which (re)invention and consolidation of power relations are important.[21]

With the advancement of information and communication through the smartphone and the possibilities of receiving, using, and engaging social media, a new dynamic has brought socio-political change. For the youth in central Chad, this was revealed in 2009 when the smartphone became widespread. Among young people in central Mali, we saw an enormous growth in smartphones in 2012. In general, anno 2017, the smartphone covers enormous terrain, though it is still confined to a relatively small group in most countries where I do research.[22]

Can we compare this 'information work' with the notion of 'radio trottoir' introduced by Stephen Ellis in an article in 1989?[23] He defines radio trottoir as news traveling without a hierarchical node where news is created. The main participants in this digital 'pavement radio' are youth.

For instance, this Facebook post (Figure 8) references the torture of youth in a Ndjaména prison after their arrest during a protest in 2015. The video of children being tortured in prison held the state responsible and leading politicians could not escape the consequences. Protests

Figure 8: Facebook post, Chad (picture: Mirjam de Bruijn 2015).

followed and meant a new step in the development of youth movements in Chad. This is an example of a moment of citizen journalism that changed, at least temporarily, the political scene in Chad.

A note on how this 'information work' on the pavement can also be devastating. It is full of rumors, of fake films, of creations to convince people of a cause. For instance, the videos circulating during the conflicts in the Central African Republic in 2013, 2014, and today have upset the social fabric, infusing religious contradictions and exacerbating violence. Videos that were circulated via WhatsApp between October and November 2016 in Cameroon were apparently fake, using footage from other areas and past events to create an image of terror and violence occurring at that time in Cameroon. The news is often manipulated, also on social media.

There is no doubt that YouTube, Facebook, Instagram, imo, and, more recently, WhatsApp have become connectors not only of short messages but of complete information flows, discussion forums, videos, and audio messages where politics and the social take on new forms and interpretations. These are places where people, especially urban youth and urbanized rural youth, unite with the diaspora and friends all over the world. Places where money flows have become digitized (mobile money innovations), and access to websites and blogs have become a reality. These media are democratic and hybrid, they are ad hoc, they are flexible and dynamic, and they are difficult to control. Although it may indeed still be a small proportion of the population that uses smartphones, they have tremendous potential to influence socio-political life.

This image of a phone booth in central Chad, taken in 2009, epitomizes this new information technology; it carries messages and informs meaning. The technology creates new possibilities of sharing information that are encompassed by the concepts of 'citizen journalism', 'citizen science', and 'citizen alerts'.[24] The phone booth sends messages with its colors and posters, as well as the information received at the booth. As of 2017, the smartphone and social media have basically downsized such telephone booths into a pocket-size (information) package which has complex effects.

ANDROID YOUTH

On February 10, 2016, Youth Day, Cameroonian president Paul Biya addressed the nation with a speech introducing the concept of an 'Android Generation'.[25] The Android Generation is innovative and lives with and in the digital economy that is the future of the nation. The compliments and positive remarks in this speech were denounced by the media, including social media. Interestingly, the terms 'Android Generation' and later 'Android Youth' have been accepted as concepts. It is highly ironic that Paul Biya decided to disable internet service and deny the Android Youth their development in anglophone Cameroon as a result of protests in the fall of 2016. Although the concept and denouncement of the Android Youth may be discussed, the socio-political changes brought by smartphones and social media are undebatable, which I would like to illustrate with two examples.

Figure 9: Phone booth ('call box') with an Obama poster in central Chad, Mongo (picture: Mirjam de Bruijn 2009).

URBAN YOUTH

Increasingly, it is the urban Android Youth who are leading protest movements in various cities in Senegal, Burkina-Faso, Chad, and the Democratic Republic of Congo, among others.[26] In his speech on February 10, 2017 after the protests and revolts in anglophone Cameroon, the discourse of Paul Biya had completely changed; he now saw these Android Youth as irresponsible and called for a renewal of their patriotism. That these protests were actually well organized through SMS, messenger, and phone calls by the same Android Youth he had praised for their entrepreneurship and innovation only a year before was conveniently ignored. In 2016, we photographed this banner in the streets of Yaoundé where the government of Cameroon warned against the 'dangers' of the internet generation (see Figure 10).

The youth protests were informed by the news, messages, analysis, and exchanges carried by smartphones as part of the 'information work' affecting the trajectory of political development. Increasingly, the authoritarian states of Chad, Cameroon, and Mali react accordingly. In Chad, the internet was disabled after the presidential elections on April 10, 2016, in Cameroon after the fall 2016 protests in the north-west, and in Mali after youth protested changes to the constitution in the spring of 2017. These reactions show how powerful 'information work' through new technology is. As a friend in Chad said, "la peur a changé du camp", meaning that governments are increasingly aware of the power of this medium of communication.

Figure 10: Banner in the streets of Yaounde (picture: Mirjam de Bruijn 2016).

RURAL MALI: NOMADS UNITE

The power of new communication technologies can also be felt in rural areas, such as central Mali.[27] In 2012, northern Mali was gripped by the Tamashek uprising that was later hijacked by Jihadi oriented movements. In 2013, the French stabilized the region and chased the so-called Jihadi occupiers out. This operation was followed by a UN mission. The UN mission did not really consider central Mali to be part of the battlefield and, as such, did not station troops there. They were wrong and that decision left the population of central Mali unprotected and insecure. Today, central Mali is one of the most insecure and conflict-ridden regions in the Sahel.

Ahmadou, the herdsman who called me at breakfast in 2006, is now in a situation where he no longer knows what to do or which side to choose. He is inclined to choose the Jihadi movements. It is interesting to note that 2012 was the year when mobile phone use began to intensify and when the first smartphones appeared among nomads. What was the role of the mobile telephone and smartphone in the life of Ahmadou and his fellow nomads during this period of hardship?[28] In 2012, the Jihadi occupants came with messages of security and connectivity through the mobile phone. Then, phones were filled with the words of preachers and with videos that sent clear messages of marginalization and commonality between nomads and their Muslim brothers.[29]

The nomads were drawn into armed action as a result of the state's failure to protect them, training in Jihadi camps and buying weapons. Already convinced of the need for change, the nomads mobilized their brothers via phone calls and SMS, and by traveling to unite in a nomad movement to claim their rights. Their appeals to international and national bodies for help was in vain.

This all culminated in the organization of nomads in a movement. The Android Youth joined in armed groups and in a communication network. They continued receiving sermons from increasingly fanatic preachers on their phones while the state and international community's neglect drew them into armed conflict. Today, the security situation in central Mali, the home of these nomads, has become extremely difficult to control.

The state has responded with military might and oppression. Young Fulani are the victims of discrimina-

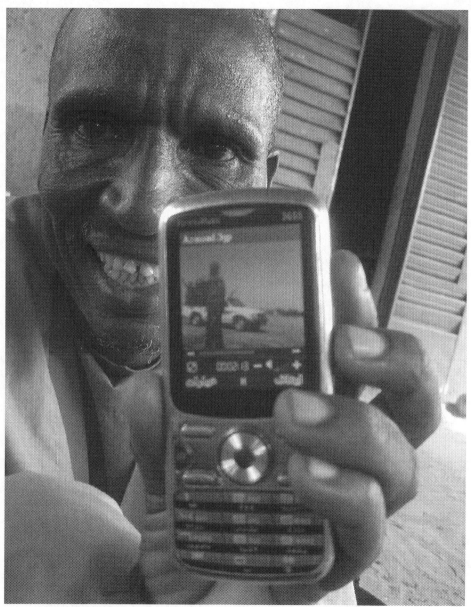

Figure 11: Ahmadou and his son's smartphone (picture: Boukary Sangaré 2013).

tion. They are depicted as Jihadi, automatically identi-
fied as such, and arrested accordingly. Their plight has
become part of a widespread protest against the situation
of the nomads that is supported by diasporic networks in
the cities, which are in regular contact with the rural
areas and keep each other informed. These city-based
Fulani, often Android Youth, also function as (sometimes deeply biased) information channels for others via,
for example, a Facebook alert site (Kisal) or (closed)
WhatsApp groups. It seems very difficult to control or
countervail this powerful connectivity that is mingled
with armed violence.

Citizen journalism, Facebook activism, and connectivity have become tools for the movements that we have
seen surface in the past five years in West and Central
Africa. Of course, underlying problems are profound and
they are not new, but it seems that information travels further and faster while the formulation of problems has a
new audience who acts accordingly. Hence, connectivity
through the internet, mobile phones, and Android Youth
have become weapons in the struggle for a different future.

I have shown that mobile telephony, smartphones,
and internet — in short, the digital — has changed societies in social, political, and also economic (unexpected)
ways. That this raises questions of where this will go is
clear from the literature that has been produced over the
past few years. Research into this digital space is still in
its infancy, methodologies are under construction, and
theories are in the making. One research direction that
we urgently need to develop is the political ecology of
digital communication.

PRACTICE OF
KNOWLEDGE PRODUCTION

The conclusions of the changing realities I have high-
lighted have consequences not only for the appearance
of new 'fields' or layers in the study of African societies
but also for the way we researchers 'do' this. Information
flows, pavement, and digitized radio trottoir are immedi-
ately reflected in our academic practices.[30]

Let us return to 1990 when I began my PhD fieldwork
in Mali. At that time, the nearest telephone was a three-
hour drive from the nomad's camp where we were stay-
ing, and the only public phone to be found was in the
post office. That was then. We wrote a book on nomads
and how they cope with insecurity, as well as translating
lyrics about the region's history told to us by a bard.
Once published, these texts were kept in repositories, indeed well read by a community of scholars interested in
the Sahel and Fulani. Today these texts have been digitized, and they have also been read by educated elites
from the Fulani groups we worked with. The texts have
been integrated into the debates on Fulani and their supposed implications in Jihadism today. Parts of our conclusions enter the discussion with members of the UN
mission in Mali. Other books on the Fulani are also traveling in the digital sphere, some of them relating Fulani
origins to Ethiopia and a heroic memory of Jihadism.
These ideas take center stage in Fulani statements that
defend their cause to the international community.

We, the authors of some of these works, have become
a part of these discussions anew. We cannot maintain an
outsider's position. Discussions on Facebook and ex-

changes on phones are a part of the pavement where our topics of research are discussed. This is a form of co-creation and a use of our texts that is not steered by us. However, we must now step in and join in this creation. The digital environment and new communication possibilities have changed our position; we cannot *not* be engaged.

In the practice of present-day research, these dynamics are at the forefront. The educated elites and the Android Youth are participants in our research field, both informing us about the field and sharing their analyses. They 'work' with us on the information that will fill future books. I started this lecture by stating that our 'informants' will become co-creators. The digital environment and connectivity it entails will force academics who work 'on' Africa to change their attitude to work instead 'with' Africa, as well as the other way around. This form of co-creation will allow the observers and readers to see what the knowledge produced in this interaction is all about. It will give credit to the co-creators in the process of joint knowledge production about Africa and African relations. Such forms of knowledge creation will not only construct shared knowledge, they will also make qualitative methods[31] of research more transparent. They will help to find solutions to the hierarchization of knowledge problem, which is enveloped in the debate on the decolonization of knowledge production.[32]

Probably I am too optimistic as the working environment in the digital is not yet optimal. Skype does not always work, Virtual Research Environments do not work in many places in Africa, and the digitization of materials is still in process. During a meeting of the project Common Lab Research Infrastructure for the Arts and Humanities (CLARIAH), we discussed data mining as an important tool for research. However, it became clear that data mining as a tool for research harbors the risk of excluding Africa, where datasets are still in the making, from knowledge production.

Is it possible to construct the academy by means of multiple voices, layered but not hierarchical?

TO DREAM AND TO REALIZE

The images of disconnected Africa and the digital divide persist in maps circulating via the internet and displayed in classrooms. The digital divide that is shown might give the impression that the stories I presented avove are fantasies, that my ideas about collaboration and co-creation are science-fiction.

However, I hope that my stories have shown that there is a lot more than these maps show. Maps of digital connectivity are usually based on statistics from the fixed net, not taking into account smartphones and their mobile internet connectivity.

African societies are mobile and it is mobile devices that will help to achieve the socio-political change needed for the well-being of so many. These devices may well be an alternative for longed for infrastructures such as well-equipped hospitals, libraries, and easy money transfers, to name a few. Digital innovations like mobile money or mobile health are innovations that seem to have a future in Africa. The future is to work together with the many technology and innovation hubs in Africa.

Why not develop mobile libraries, archives, memories, and possibilities for serious 'information work' so that we can indeed co-create a knowledge economy in which African youth in all their diversity, both rural and urban, can find their way. This will be the true revolution of the digital.

Of course, we should follow these developments while keeping an eye on the possible negative effects, such as the control of the state, new processes of exclusion, or the reproduction rather than the dismantling of hierarchical relations in knowledge production. These developments were also part of my talk and should be considered in the future research and practices that we develop.

This is where I am in my journey into the digital and Africa. It is time that we Africanists take up the challenge and use the digital humanities, digital anthropology, and digital African studies as platforms to discuss a true and deep transformation of knowledge production.

ENDNOTES

1   See https://www.mobileafricarevisited.wordpress.com (accessed
    June 15, 2018) and www.connecting-in-times-of-duress.nl (accessed
    June 15, 2018).
2   The discussion I provoke in this lecture is also a continuation of
    the scholarly work of my colleagues in: Barringer, T., & Wallace,
    M. (Eds.) (2014). *African Studies in the digital age: DisConnects?*
    Leiden: Brill. See also the result of intensive collaborative work at
    the African Studies Centre Leiden in: De Bruijn, M., & van Dijk,
    R. (Eds.) (2012), *The social life of connectivity in Africa.*
    Basingstoke: Palgrave Macmillan.
3   This argument was inspired by the research program 'Connecting in
    times of duress' and 'Voice4Thought', an artistic-academic project
    at voice4thought.org (accessed June 15, 2018).
4   See 'Briding humanities', an open access academic e-publishing
    platform that experiments with co-creation and digital methodolo-
    gies at www.bridginghumanities.nl (accessed June 15, 2018).
5   See a short video of Cameroonians discussing the mobile phone, its
    use, and what the phone means to them in their life: eyesees/ASC.
    (Sijsma, S., & de Bruijn, M.) (2008). *Cameroonians about phones*
    [Streaming Video]. Available from https://mobileafricarevisited.
    wordpress.com/short-movies-phones-in-africa/ (accessed June 15,
    2018). This video was made for a project with the Information Age
    Gallery at the Science Museum, London. See: Blyth, T. (Ed.) 2014.
    Information age: Six networks that changed our world. London:
    Scala Arts & Heritage.
6   The future of the telephone. *Scientific American,* 1880. Cited in
    J. Gleick (2011), The Information: A history, a theory, a flood.
    New York: Pantheon Books.
7   For a complete report, see: https://mobileafricarevisited.wordpress.
    com/wotro-final-report/ (accessed June 15, 2018).
8   Gitelman L., & Pingree G.B. (2003). Introduction: What's new
    about new media? In L. Gitelman & G.B. Pingree (Eds.), *New
    media, 1740–1915* (pp. xi–xxii). Cambridge: MIT Press.
9   de Bruijn, M. (September 2008). *"The telephone has grown legs":
    Mobile communication and social change in the margins of African
    society.* Inaugural lecture for the acceptance of Professorship at
    Leiden University. Retrieved from https://openaccess.leidenuniv.nl/
    handle/1887/17793 (accessed June 15, 2018).
10 It subscribes to the main items referred to in globalization theories.
11 See, for example, Overseas Development Institute Briefing Paper

33. (January 2018). *Pro-poor growth and development: Linking economic growth and poverty reduction.* Retrieved from https://www.odi.org/sites/odi.org.uk/files/odi-assets/publications-opinion-files/825.pdf (accessed June 15, 2018).

12 For insight into the way the mobile phone has altered the Sudanese landscape, the business around phones, and the companies behind them, see: eyesees/ASC. (Sijsma, S., & de Bruijn, M.). (2008). *The wireless camel* [Video stream]. Available from https://mobileafrica revisited.wordpress.com/short-movies-phones-in-africa/ (accessed June 15, 2018).

13 Hahn, H., & Kibora, L. (2008). The domestication of the mobile phone: Oral society and new ICT in Burkina Faso. *The Journal of Modern African Studies,* 46(1), 87–109.

14 During these first years, we did research into mobile communication in Mali, Chad, and Cameroon. Information available at: http://mobileafricarevisited.wordpress.com (accessed June 15, 2018). See also: Seli, D. (2013). *(Dé)connexions identitaires hadjeray: Les enjeux des technologies de la communication au Tchad.* Cameroon: Langaa.; Nyamnjoh, H.M. (2014). *Bridging mobilities: ICTs appro-priation by Cameroonians in South Africa and the Netherlands.* Cameroon: Langaa.; Keita, N., Magassa, S., Sangaré, B., & Rhissa, Y.A. (2015). *Téléphonie et mobilité au Mali.* Cameroon: Langaa.; Sangaré, B. (2010). *Peuls et mobilité dans le cercle de Douentza: l'espace social et la téléphonie mobile en question* (MA thesis). Université de Bamako, Bamako, Mali.; de Bruijn, M., Nyamnjoh, F., Brinkman, I. (Eds.). (2009). *Mobile phones: The new talking drums of everyday Africa.* Leiden/Cameroon: ASC /Langaa.

15 Granovetter, M.S. (1973). The strength of weak ties. *The American Journal of Sociology,* 78(6), 1360–1380.

16 de Bruijn, M., & Brinkman, I. (2011). "Communicating Africa". Researching mobile kin communities, communication technologies, and social transformation in Angola and Cameroon. *Autrepart,* 1–2(57/58), 41–57.

17 de Bruijn, M., Nyamnjoh, F., & Angwafo, P. (2010). Mobile inter-connections: Reinterpreting distance, relating and difference in the Cameroonian Grassfields. *Journal of African Media,* 2(3), 267–285.; Archambault, J.S. (2012). 'Travelling while sitting down': Mobile phones, mobility and the communication landscape in Inhambane, Mozambique. *Africa* 82(3), 393–412.; van Beek, W. (2009). The healer and his phone: Medicinal dynamics among the Kapsiki/Higi of North Cameroon. In M. de Bruijn, F. Nyamnjoh, & I. Brinkman (Eds.), *Mobile phones: The new talking drums of everyday Africa* (pp. 125–133). Leiden:ASC/Langaa.

18 Jidenma, N. (2013, November 7). The real mobile revolution: Africa's smartphone future. CNN. Retrieved from http://edition.cnn.com/2013/11/07/opinion/real-mobile-revolution-africa-smartphone/index.html (accessed June 15, 2018).
19 Gleick, J. (2011). *The Information: A history, a theory, a flood.* New York: Pantheon Books.
20 Fabian, J. (2003). Forgetful remembering: A colonial life in the Congo. *Africa* 73(4), 489–504.
21 Castells, M. (2009). *Communication power.* Oxford: Oxford University Press.
22 The average of 3% in Chad (survey result of population with smart-phones), however, still represents a lot of people.
23 Ellis, S. (1989). Tuning in to pavement radio. *African Affairs,* 88(352), 321–330.
24 Mutsvairo, B. (Ed.). (2016). *Participatory politics and citizen journalism in a networked Africa: A connected continent.* Basingstoke: Palgrave Macmillan.
25 "In addition, there is another domain which I know you of the so-called 'Android' generation hold most dear, namely the development of the digital economy." Biya, P. (2016, February 10). 50th edition of the Youth Day: Head of State's message to the youth. Retrieved from https://www.prc.cm/en/news/speeches-of-the-president/1651-50th-edition-of-the-youth-day-head-of-state-s-message-to-the-youth (accessed June 15, 2018).
26 The third revolution seems to be present, as was argued in the book: Branch, A., Mampilly, Z. (2015). *Africa uprising: Popular protest and political change.* London: Zed Books.
27 We followed the situation in Mali closely, especially through the eyes of Boukary Sangaré, a PhD student, and through contact by phone, internet, or Facebook exchanges and posts. (Sangaré, 2010). Since 2016 we have worked on a research project in the area. For more information, visit: http://www.ascleiden.nl/research/projects/nomads-facing-change-political-mobilisation-among-sahelian-pastoralists (accessed June 15, 2018).
See also two blog texts by Mirjam de Bruijn: https://mirjamdebruijn.wordpress.com/2015/05/04/ahmadou-a-nomad-leader-in-mali/ (accessed June 15, 2018) and https://mirjamdebruijn.wordpress.com/2015/10/12/quest-for-citizenship-of-the-fulbe-seminomads-in-central-mali (accessed June 15, 2018).
See also: Lecocq, B., Mann, G., Whitehouse, B., Pelckmans, L., & Badi, D. (2013). One hippopotamus and eight blind analysts:

A multivocal analysis of the 2012 political crisis in the divided Republic of Mali. *Review of African Political Economy,* 40(137), 343–357.

28 Keita, N., Magassa, S., Sangaré, B., & Rhissa, Y.A. (2015). *Téléphonie et mobilité au Mali.* Cameroon: Langaa.

29 Modibo Cissé, 2018 (forthcoming).

30 I will not further the 'effect' on libraries nor on data archiving. For effects on information collections, see: Barringer, T., & Wallace, M. (Eds.). (2014). *African studies in the digital age: DisConnects?* Leiden: Brill.

31 Qualitative methods of research could be put in relation to quantitative 'big data' science, which continues to exert its influence and needs to be complemented with more context-sensitive qualitative studies.

32 To understand African realities and histories, we need to allow multiple voices to join in the creation of knowledge. An example is a project I started with a group of academics, film-makers, and artists in the Netherlands, France, and West and Central Africa called Voice4thought (see: www.voice4thought.org). This led us to develop an e-platform/journal that develops methods for multimedia publications called Briding Humanities (see: www.bridginghumanities.com).

CARL SCHLETTWEIN LECTURES

The distinguished lecture of the Centre for African Studies Basel is held in remembrance of Dr h.c. Carl Schlettwein, who played an important part in the development of African Studies at Basel and in the establishment of our Centre. His moral support was supplemented by the generous and farsighted assistance he gave to these activities. Carl Schlettwein was born in Mecklenburg in 1925 and emigrated to South Africa in 1952. Until 1963 he lived in South West Africa, the former German colony that was then under South African administration. When he married Daniela Gsell he moved to Basel. In 1971 Schlettwein founded the Basler Afrika Bibliographien (BAB) as a library and publishing house in order to allow international institutions to access bibliographic information on South West Africa (Namibia). Accordingly, he published the first national bibliography on this African country. Through these activities the BAB contributed to documenting and researching a nation with a particularly difficult history. Other publications dealt with historical, literary and geo-methodological topics, and included titles on Swiss-African relations. From an individualistic private initiative, the BAB developed into an institution open to the public and became a cornerstone of the Centre for African Studies Basel. As the Namibia Resource Centre—Southern Africa Library the institution is of world-wide importance. The Carl Schlettwein Stiftung, which was founded in 1994, runs the BAB and supports students and projects in Namibia as well as in other Southern African countries. In 2001, the Carl Schlettwein Foundation funded the establishment of the Chair of African History, providing the basis for today's professorship in African History and the African Studies programme at the University of Basel. The Foundation works closely with the Centre for African Studies Basel to provide support for teaching and research and in 2016 it enabled the Centre to establish a position on Namibian and Southern African Studies. The University of Basel honoured Carl Schlettwein with an honorary doctorate in 1997.

Printed in the United States
By Bookmasters